CW00502138

The complete paleo diet cookbook

PALEO-FRIENDLY RECIPES TO START A NEW WHOLE FOODS LIFESTYLE

-Jaylee Beck-

TABLE OF CONTENTS:

CHAPTER 1: **BREAKFAST**

EGGS POACHED IN TOMATO JUICE

Prep:

10 mins

Cook:

1 hr 15 mins

Total:

1 hr 25 mins

Servings:

4

Yield:

4 servings

INGREDIENTS:

2 tablespoons olive oil, or to taste

½ onion, finely chopped

2 cloves garlic, finely chopped

8 cups tomato sauce

¼ cup dry red wine, or more to taste

1 tablespoon dried parsley

1 tablespoon dried basil

1 tablespoon dried oregano

½ teaspoon salt

¼ teaspoon freshly ground black pepper, or more to taste

1 bay leaf, or more to taste

1 pinch red pepper flakes

8 eggs

DIRECTIONS:

1

Heat olive oil in a large skillet over medium heat. Cook and stir onion and garlic in hot oil until tender, about 5 minutes.

2

Stir tomato sauce, red wine, parsley, basil, oregano, salt, pepper, bay leaf, and red pepper flakes with the onion and garlic; bring to a simmer, reduce heat to low, and cook until the sauce has thickened, about 45 minutes.

3

Crack eggs into a bowl one at a time and gently slide them into the tomato sauce; cook until beginning to firm, 2 to 3 minutes. Spoon sauce over the eggs to cover. Place a lid on the skillet and simmer until sauce has thickened, about 30 minutes.

NUTRITION FACTS:

354 calories; protein 19.9g; carbohydrates 32.1g; fat 17.8g;

CHICKEN AND WAFFLES

Prep:

15 mins

Cook:

30 mins

Additional:

20 mins

Total:

1 hr 5 mins

Servings:

4

Yield:

4 sandwiches

INGREDIENTS:

4 eggs

¼ cup heavy cream

2 tablespoons cayenne pepper

1 tablespoon salt

1 tablespoon ground black pepper

2 cups all-purpose flour

1 cup cornstarch

1 tablespoon salt

1 quart peanut oil for frying

8 chicken tenders

1 cup mayonnaise

¼ cup maple syrup

2 teaspoons prepared horseradish

1 teaspoon dry mustard powder

12 slices bacon

8 thin slices Cheddar cheese

8 plain frozen waffles

DIRECTIONS:

1

Whisk together the eggs, cream, cayenne pepper, 1 tablespoon salt, and black pepper in a large bowl. In a paper bag, shake together the flour, cornstarch, and 1 tablespoon salt.

2

Dip the chicken into the beaten egg mixture, then place into the flour mixture and shake to coat. Place the breaded chicken onto a wire rack; do not stack. Let the chicken rest for 20 minutes to allow the coating to set.

3

Heat about 3 inches of oil in a deep-fryer or large saucepan to 375 degrees F (190 degrees C). In small batches, fry chicken 5 to 8 minutes until golden brown. Remove chicken, and drain on paper towels. Set aside or keep warm in a a low oven.

4

Combine the mayonnaise, maple syrup, horseradish, and mustard powder in a medium bowl. Place the bacon in a large, deep skillet, and cook over medium-high heat, turning occasionally, until evenly browned, about 10 minutes. Drain the bacon slices on a paper towel-lined plate.

5

To assemble the sandwiches: Place 4 waffles on a cookie sheet, top each waffle with 2 chicken tenders, 3 slices of bacon, and 2 slices of Cheddar. Broil the sandwich for a 3 to 5 minutes until the cheese melts. Spread 3 tablespoons of the maple mayonnaise on the remaining 4 waffles and place on top of the sandwich.

NUTRITION FACTS:

1793 calories; protein 72.9g; carbohydrates 127.1g; fat 109.9g

SCRAMBLED EGG WITH ZUCCHINI

Prep:

10 mins

Cook:

15 mins

Total:

25 mins

Servings:

4

Yield:

4 servings

INGREDIENTS:

4 eggs, lightly beaten

2 tablespoons grated Parmesan cheese

2 tablespoons olive oil

1 zucchini, sliced 1/8- to 1/4-inch thick

garlic powder, or to taste

salt and ground black pepper to taste

DIRECTIONS:

1

Stir the eggs and Parmesan cheese together in a bowl; set aside.

2

Heat the olive oil in a large skillet over medium-high heat; cook the zucchini in the hot oil until softened and lightly browned, about 7 minutes. Season the zucchini with garlic powder, salt, and pepper. Reduce heat to medium; pour the egg mixture into the skillet. Cook, stirring gently, for about 3 minutes. Remove the skillet from the heat and cover. Keep covered off the heat until the eggs set, about 2 minutes more.

NUTRITION FACTS:

147 calories; protein 7.6g; carbohydrates 1.6g; fat 12.5g

PALEO PANCAKES

Prep:

15 mins

Cook:

10 mins

Total:

25 mins

Servings:

2

Yield:

2 servings

INGREDIENTS:

1 banana, mashed

3 eggs

¼ cup almond flour

1 tablespoon almond butter

1 teaspoon vanilla extract

½ teaspoon ground cinnamon

⅛ teaspoon baking soda

⅛ teaspoon baking powder

1 teaspoon olive oil, or as needed

DIRECTIONS:

1

Whisk banana, eggs, almond flour, almond butter, vanilla extract, cinnamon, baking soda, and baking powder together in a bowl until batter is smooth.

2

Heat olive oil on a griddle or skillet over medium-high heat. Drop batter by large spoonfuls onto the griddle and cook until bubbles form and the edges are dry, 3 to 4 minutes. Flip and cook until browned on the other side, 2 to 3 minutes. Repeat with remaining batter.

NUTRITION FACTS:

330 calories; protein 14.6g; carbohydrates 19.9g; fat 22.5g;

BUTTERNUT SQUASH PALEO PORRIDGE

Prep:

10 mins

Cook:

50 mins

Total:

1 hr

Servings:

3

Yield:

3 servings

INGREDIENTS:

1 butternut squash, halved and seeded

water as needed

¼ cup coconut milk, or to taste

½ teaspoon ground cinnamon

1 tablespoon chopped walnuts

DIRECTIONS:

1

Preheat oven to 350 degrees F (175 degrees C).

2

Place butternut squash halves, cut-side up, in a baking dish; fill dish with 1/4 inch of water.

3

Bake in the preheated oven until softened, 50 to 60 minutes. Cool squash.

4

Scoop squash flesh into a bowl and mash with a fork or potato masher until smooth. Stir coconut milk and cinnamon into squash; top with walnuts.

NUTRITION FACTS:

242 calories; protein 4.9g; carbohydrates 49.9g; fat 6g

SWEET BREAKFAST HASH WITH APPLE AND ROSEMARY

Prep:

15 mins

Cook:

20 mins

Total:

35 mins

Servings:

6

Yield:

6 servings

INGREDIENTS:

2 tablespoons olive oil

3 medium russet potatoes, diced

½ medium sweet onion, chopped

1 (12 ounce) package sweet chicken sausage links diced

1 Golden Delicious apple - peeled, cored, and diced

½ cup dried cranberries (Optional)

1 teaspoon salt

1 teaspoon ground black pepper

½ teaspoon ground fennel seeds

½ teaspoon chopped fresh rosemary

¼ teaspoon red pepper flakes

DIRECTIONS:

1

Heat oil in a large saute pan over medium-high heat. Add potatoes and onion and cook until potatoes are slightly brown and onions are translucent, 12 to 15 minutes.

2

Heat a small saute pan over medium-high heat. Saute sausage, apple, cranberries, salt, black pepper, fennel, rosemary, and red pepper flakes for 5 minutes. Add to potato mixture and serve.

NUTRITION FACTS:

261 calories; protein 12.4g; carbohydrates 32.3g; fat 9.3g;

CRAB CAKES

Prep:

40 mins

Cook:

10 mins

Additional:

1 hr

Total:

1 hr 50 mins

Servings:

4

Yield:

4 large crab cakes

INGREDIENTS:

2 tablespoons margarine

½ cup minced onion

½ cup minced green bell pepper

1 tablespoon dry mustard

1 teaspoon Worcestershire sauce

1 teaspoon seafood seasoning

¾ teaspoon salt

¼ teaspoon hot pepper sauce

¼ teaspoon ground black pepper

1 pinch cayenne pepper

¼ cup all-purpose flour

1 ¼ cups light cream

1 pound crab meat

2 egg yolks, beaten

½ cup bread crumbs

1 tablespoon melted butter

½ teaspoon paprika

1 cup corn oil, or as needed

DIRECTIONS:

1

Melt margarine in a skillet over medium heat. Cook and stir onion and green bell pepper in margarine until tender, about 5 minutes. Stir mustard, Worcestershire sauce, seafood seasoning, salt, hot pepper sauce, black pepper, and cayenne pepper into the onion mixture. Sprinkle flour over the mixture; stir to integrate. Pour cream over the mixture; bring to a boil, stirring constantly and cook for 1 minute. Fold crab meat into the mixture.

2

Spoon some of the liquid from the skillet into the bowl with the beaten egg yolks to temper the egg; stir. Pour the egg mixture into the skillet and stir. Cook, stirring constantly, until the mixture thickens, about 5 minutes.

3

Transfer crab mixture to a bowl; refrigerate until chilled completely, about 1 hour.

4

Mix bread crumbs, melted butter, and paprika in a shallow bowl.

5

Divide the crab mixture into 4 portions; form into patties. Gently press the patties into the bread crumb mixture to coat.

6

Pour enough corn oil into a flat-bottomed pan to be 1-inch deep; heat to 350 degrees F (175 degrees C).

7

Cook patties in hot oil until golden brown, 2 to 3 minutes per side.

NUTRITION FACTS:
326 calories; protein 25.6g; carbohydrates 25.4g; fat 13.3g;

EGG,CHEESE, AND TURKEY BREAKFAST BURRITO

Prep:

15 mins

Cook:

15 mins

Total:

30 mins

Servings:

10

Yield:

10 burritos

INGREDIENTS:

10 egg whites

6 eggs

2 teaspoons vegetable oil, or as needed, divided

½ (16 ounce) package frozen hash brown potatoes, thawed

½ pound ground turkey

1 cup chopped red onion

6 slices hickory ham diced

1 ½ cups shredded fat-free Cheddar cheese

10 low-carb, high-fiber tortillas, warmed

DIRECTIONS:

1

Whisk egg whites and eggs together in a large bowl.

2

Heat 1 teaspoon oil in a large frying pan over medium-high heat. Cook and stir hash browns until browned and crispy, about 5 minutes. Transfer hash browns to a large bowl.

3

Heat 1 teaspoon oil in the same frying pan over medium heat. Add turkey, onion, and ham. Cook and stir until turkey is crumbly and onion softens, about 5 minutes. Add eggs; stir until scrambled and set, 5 to 7 minutes. Add cheese and let melt, about 3 minutes. Pour mixture into the bowl with the hash browns. Mix everything together.

4

Plate tortillas. Add about 3 tablespoons of filling to each tortilla. Fold opposing edges of a tortilla to overlap the filling. Roll 1 of the opposing edges around the filling, creating a burrito. Repeat for remaining tortillas.

NUTRITION FACTS:
261 calories; protein 25.5g; carbohydrates 21.6g; fat 12.6g;

CHAPTER 2: LUNCH

EGGPLANT GRATIN

Prep:

15 mins

Cook:

45 mins

Additional:

20 mins

Total:

1 hr 20 mins

Servings:

4

Yield:

4 servings

INGREDIENTS:

4 eggplants

salt and freshly ground black pepper to taste

1 (8 ounce) package feta cheese

1 cup heavy whipping cream

3 cloves garlic, minced

1 tablespoon chopped fresh parsley, or more to taste

1 tablespoon chopped fresh basil, or more to taste

1 splash olive oil

4 ripe tomatoes, sliced

2 yellow bell peppers, chopped

DIRECTIONS:

1

Slice eggplants in such a way that the slices are still connected at the bottom. Sprinkle with salt and set aside for 20 minutes. Wash off salt under running cold water and pat dry.

2

Preheat oven to 400 degrees F (200 degrees C). Grease a baking dish.

3

Mash feta cheese and cream together with a fork. Mix in garlic, parsley, basil, olive oil, salt, and pepper.

4

Place eggplants with the cut-side up into the prepared baking dish. Arrange tomato slices and bell pepper pieces alternately in between the eggplant slices. Pour feta-mixture over eggplants and cover with aluminum foil.

5

Bake in the preheated oven until feta cheese is melted and eggplants are cooked through, about 45 minutes. Sprinkle with more parsley.

NUTRITION FACTS:

549 calories; protein 17g; carbohydrates 46.7g; fat 36.8g;

TOMATO MEATBALLS

Prep:

20 mins

Cook:

15 mins

Total:

35 mins

Servings:

4

Yield:

4 servings

INGREDIENTS:

3 tablespoons water

3 sun-dried tomatoes, finely chopped

1 pound ground beef

¼ onion, minced

½ cup bread crumbs

¼ cup half-and-half

freshly ground black pepper to taste

sea salt to taste

2 tablespoons olive oil

1 cup cold water

2 tablespoons cornstarch

DIRECTIONS:

1

Combine the water and tomatoes in a small saucepan over medium heat; cook until the water is absorbed.

2

Mix together the tomatoes, ground beef, onion, bread crumbs, half-and-half, salt, and pepper in a bowl. Form the mixture into golf ball-sized spheres.

3

Heat the olive oil in a skillet over medium heat. Cook the meatballs in the heated oil until no longer pink in the center, turning several times to maintain even coloring; remove and set aside, reserving drippings in the skillet. Stir the water and cornstarch together to dissolve cornstarch, then mix into the drippings. Replace skillet over medium heat, bring to a boil and stir until thickened; serve on side of meatballs.

NUTRITION FACTS:
510 calories; protein 21.5g; carbohydrates 16.3g; fat 39.4g;

STEAMED CLAMS IN BUTTER AND SAKE

Prep:

10 mins

Cook:

10 mins

Additional:

5 mins

Total:

25 mins

Servings:

4

Yield:

4 servings

INGREDIENTS:

4 teaspoons sake

4 teaspoons mirin (Japanese sweet wine)

2 teaspoons rice vinegar

1 ¼ pounds clams in shell, scrubbed

3 tablespoons butter

1 teaspoon soy sauce

1 green onion, chopped

DIRECTIONS:

1

Scrub and rinse clams. Soak in a large bowl of cold water for 5 minutes. Drain thoroughly.

2

Heat a wok or large saucepan over high heat. Quickly pour in the sake, mirin and rice vinegar. Add the clams; cover and cook until the clams open, 3 to 4 minutes. Discard any clams that do not open.

3

Remove any scum that forms on the surface using a spoon or paper towel. Stir in the butter, soy sauce and green onion, tossing to coat the clams as the butter melts. Arrange clams on a serving plate and drizzle the sauce over them. Serve immediately.

NUTRITION FACTS:
21 calories; protein 4.5g; carbohydrates 3g; fat 9g;

QUICK ZUCCHINI NOODLES WITH PESTO

Prep:
25 mins
Total:
25 mins
Servings:
2
Yield:
2 servings

INGREDIENTS:
3 ½ ounces Parmesan cheese, roughly chopped
¾ cup walnuts
⅓ cup olive oil, or as needed
1 bunch fresh parsley, chopped
1 clove garlic, minced
2 large zucchini, cut into noodles with a spiralizer
1 ½ pints cherry tomatoes, halved
1 cup pitted Kalamata olives, halved

DIRECTIONS:
1

Place Parmesan cheese in the bowl of a food processor; process into small crumbs. Add walnuts and process into small crumbs.

2

Heat olive oil in a large skillet over medium-high heat until hot. Stir in parsley and garlic and remove from heat. Toss zucchini noodles with the hot oil mixture and Parmesan-walnut mixture. Top with cherry tomatoes and olives to serve.

NUTRITION FACTS:

1128 calories; protein 33.8g; carbohydrates 38.1g; fat 98.9g;

PALEO TACO SALAD

Prep:
25 mins
Cook:
20 mins
Total:
45 mins
Servings:
4
Yield:
4 servings

INGREDIENTS:
2 tablespoons chili powder
2 teaspoons ground cumin
2 teaspoons garlic powder
½ teaspoon cayenne pepper
salt and ground black pepper to taste
1 pound ground beef
1 onion, diced
2 cloves garlic, minced
½ cup salsa
¼ cup sour cream
1 tablespoon lime juice
2 romaine hearts, shredded
3 cups cherry tomatoes, halved
¼ cup shredded Cheddar cheese, or to taste (Optional)
⅓ cup cilantro, chopped

DIRECTIONS:

1

Mix together chili powder, cumin, garlic powder, cayenne pepper, salt, and ground black pepper in a small bowl.

2

Heat a large skillet over medium-high heat and cook ground beef, stirring often, until the meat is crumbly, evenly browned, and no longer pink, about 10 minutes. Mix in onion and garlic; cook and stir until the onion has softened and turned translucent, about 5 minutes. Stir spice mixture into ground beef mixture and cook until fragrant, 2 to 3 more minutes.

3

Combine salsa, sour cream, and lime juice in a small bowl. To serve, spread shredded romaine lettuce onto a serving platter and top with meat mixture, salsa mixture, cherry tomatoes, Cheddar cheese, and chopped cilantr

NUTRITION FACTS:

385 calories; protein 25g; carbohydrates 18.5g; fat 24.7g;

ROASTED CARROT AND FENNEL PORK

Prep:

15 mins

Cook:

1 hr 10 mins

Total:

1 hr 25 mins

Servings:

6

Yield:

6 servings

INGREDIENTS:

1 (1 pound) pork loin

3 tablespoons honey mustard

2 tablespoons dried thyme

3 large fennel bulbs, chopped

5 carrots, chopped

1 large onion, chopped

1 tablespoon salt

½ teaspoon ground black pepper

DIRECTIONS:

1

Preheat oven to 425 degrees F (220 degrees C).

2

Rub pork loin with honey mustard and thyme.

3

Combine fennel, carrots, and onion in a 9x13-inch baking dish; season with salt and pepper.

4

Roast vegetables in the preheated oven for 45 minutes. Nestle the pork loin in the center of the vegetables and cook until pork is cooked through, about 25 minutes. An instant-read thermometer inserted into the center should read at least 145 degrees F (63 degrees C). Thinly slice the pork loin to serve.

NUTRITION FACTS:
233 calories; protein 16.2g; carbohydrates 28.3g; fat 7.9g;

AVOCADO, TUNA AND TOMATO SALAD

Prep:

15 mins

Total:

15 mins

Servings:

2

Yield:

2 servings

INGREDIENTS:

1 avocado

1 (5 ounce) can tuna, drained

1 small tomato, chopped

¼ cup crumbled feta cheese

1 jalapeno pepper, finely chopped (Optional)

1 green onion, chopped

2 cloves garlic, minced

3 tablespoons chopped fresh cilantro

2 tablespoons lime juice

salt and pepper to taste

DIRECTIONS:

1

Split avocado. Save skins and discard pit. Scoop contents into a bowl; slightly mash.

2

Mix mashed avocado, tuna, tomato, feta cheese, jalapeno pepper, green onion, feta cheese, garlic, cilantro, lime juice, salt, and pepper together in a bowl.

3

Scoop mixture back into reserved avocado skins and serve immediately or chill until serving.

NUTRITION FACTS:
338 calories; protein 23.5g; carbohydrates 14.9g; fat 22.1g;

GROUND BEEF AND VEGETABLE STEW

Prep:

25 mins

Cook:

1 hr 5 mins

Total:

1 hr 30 mins

Servings:

8

Yield:

8 servings

INGREDIENTS:

1 pound ground beef

1 small onion, finely chopped

1 clove garlic, finely chopped

4 cups water

2 tablespoons beef base

1 (8 ounce) can tomato sauce

1 tablespoon Worcestershire sauce

1 teaspoon ground black pepper

½ teaspoon celery salt

¼ teaspoon ground marjoram

5 large carrots, cut into rounds

4 medium potatoes, peeled and cubed

1 cup green beans, trimmed and cut into 1-inch pieces

3 tablespoons all-purpose flour

2 tablespoons water, or more as needed

DIRECTIONS:

1

Heat a large skillet over medium-high heat. Cook and stir ground beef, onion, and garlic in the hot skillet until beef is browned and crumbly, 5 to 7 minutes. Drain and discard grease. Add 4 cups water and beef base; stir to combine. Add tomato sauce, Worcestershire sauce, pepper, celery salt, and marjoram; bring to a simmer.

2

Add carrots and simmer for 35 minutes. Add potatoes and green beans; cook until tender, about 15 minutes.

3

Meanwhile, mix flour and 2 tablespoons water together in a small bowl until no longer lumpy, adding more water if necessary. Stir into stew and simmer until thickened, 5 to 10 minutes.

NUTRITION FACTS:
257 calories; protein 14g; carbohydrates 29.2g; fat 9.7g;

CHAPTER 3: DINNER

WRAPPED ASPARAGUS

Prep:

25 mins

Cook:

8 mins

Additional:

7 mins

Total:

40 mins

Servings:

8

Yield:

8 servings

INGREDIENTS:

1 tablespoon lemon juice

1 tablespoon olive oil

1 clove garlic, minced

16 medium fresh asparagus spears, each trimmed to 5 inches

8 thin slices Prosciutto

⅓ cup soft goat cheese

DIRECTIONS:

1

Preheat oven to 425 degrees F. Combine lemon juice, olive oil and garlic in large bowl. Add asparagus; toss to coat. Place asparagus in baking pan.

2

Bake 8 minutes, or until crisp-tender. Let cool to room temperature (about 15 minutes).

3

Cut each prosciutto slice in half lengthwise. Spread each piece with about 1 teaspoon goat cheese. Wrap each slice in a spiral around each asparagus spear. Serve immediately, or cover and refrigerate until ready to serve.

NUTRITION FACTS:
85 calories; protein 6.3g; carbohydrates 1.8g; fat 6.1g;

EGGLESS ZUCCHINI LASAGNA

Prep:

20 mins

Cook:

45 mins

Additional:

15 mins

Total:

1 hr 20 mins

Servings:

4

Yield:

4 servings

INGREDIENTS:

3 large zucchini, trimmed and cut lengthwise into long strips

2 tablespoons olive oil

1 onion, chopped

2 cloves garlic, chopped

1 cup seasoned bread crumbs

1 cup grated Parmesan cheese (Optional)

1 tablespoon Italian herb seasoning

3 cups tomato sauce

¼ cup grated Parmesan cheese, or as needed (Optional)

DIRECTIONS:

1

Preheat oven to 375 degrees F (190 degrees C). Grease a 9x12-inch baking dish.

2

Bring a large pot of water to a boil and add zucchini slices; boil for 3 minutes. Drain.

3

Heat olive oil in a skillet over medium heat and cook onion and garlic, stirring frequently, until onion is translucent, about 5 minutes.

4

Mix bread crumbs, 1 cup Parmesan cheese, and Italian herb seasoning in a bowl.

5

Spoon 3 tablespoons tomato sauce into bottom of the prepared baking dish and top with 1/3 of the zucchini slices, 1/3 of the onion-garlic mixture, and 1/3 of the crumb-Parmesan cheese mixture. Repeat layers twice more, starting with 1/2 of remaining tomato sauce and layers of zucchini, onion, and crumb mixture. End with remaining tomato sauce in a layer; sprinkle 1/4 cup Parmesan cheese over the top.

6

Bake in the preheated oven until lasagna begins to bubble, about 30 minutes.

7

Preheat oven's broiler and broil the lasagna until cheese topping is browned, 2 to 3 minutes. Let casserole stand for 15 minutes to set before serving.

NUTRITION FACTS:

389 calories; protein 19.8g; carbohydrates 45.5g; fat 16.3g;

CELERY SALAD

Prep:

10 mins

Additional:

30 mins

Total:

40 mins

Servings:

2

Yield:

2 servings

INGREDIENTS:

¾ cup sliced celery

⅓ cup dried sweet cherries

⅓ cup frozen green peas, thawed

3 tablespoons chopped fresh parsley

1 tablespoon chopped pecans, toasted

1 ½ tablespoons fat-free mayonnaise

1 ½ tablespoons plain low-fat yogurt

1 ½ teaspoons fresh lemon juice

⅛ teaspoon salt

⅛ teaspoon ground black pepper

DIRECTIONS:

1

In a medium bowl, combine the celery, cherries, peas, parsley and pecans. Stir in the mayonnaise, yogurt and lemon juice. Season with salt and pepper. Chill before serving.

NUTRITION FACTS:

150 calories; protein 4.1g; carbohydrates 26.5g; fat 3g;

CAULIFLOWER STUFFING

Prep:

15 mins

Cook:

25 mins

Total:

40 mins

Servings:

8

Yield:

8 servings

INGREDIENTS:

12 ounces sage-flavored bulk pork sausage

2 tablespoons butter

1 medium onion, chopped

2 ribs celery, sliced

6 button mushrooms, sliced

¼ cup chopped carrots

1 (2 pound) head cauliflower, cut into small florets

½ cup chicken broth

¼ cup freshly chopped parsley

½ teaspoon dried thyme leaves

salt and ground black pepper to taste

DIRECTIONS:

1

Place sausage into a large skillet and cook over medium-high heat until browned and crumbly, about 5 minutes. Add butter, then stir in onion, celery, mushrooms, and carrots; cook for 5 more minutes.

2

Mix in cauliflower, broth, parsley, thyme, salt, and pepper. Cover and cook 10 minutes. Uncover and cook until liquid is absorbed, about 5 more minutes.

NUTRITION FACTS:
175 calories; protein 8.8g; carbohydrates 9.2g; fat 12.1g;

OKRA PATTIES

Prep:

20 mins

Cook:

10 mins

Total:

30 mins

Servings:

6

Yield:

6 servings

INGREDIENTS:

3 cups vegetable oil for frying

1 pound okra, finely chopped

1 cup finely chopped onion

1 teaspoon salt

¼ teaspoon pepper

½ cup water

1 egg

½ cup all-purpose flour

1 teaspoon baking powder

½ cup cornmeal

DIRECTIONS:

1

Heat 1 inch of oil in a large skillet to 375 degrees F (190 degrees C).

2

In a large bowl, mix together the okra, onion, salt, pepper, water and egg. Combine the flour, baking powder and cornmeal; and stir that into the okra mixture.

3

Carefully drop spoonfuls of the okra batter into the hot oil, and fry on each side until golden, about 2 minutes per side. Remove with a slotted spoon, and drain on paper towels.

NUTRITION FACTS:

224 calories; protein 4.8g; carbohydrates 25.1g; fat 12.3g;

CAPERS AND HALIBUT

Prep:

10 mins

Cook:

15 mins

Total:

25 mins

Servings:

4

Yield:

2 steaks

INGREDIENTS:

1 tablespoon olive oil

2 (8 ounce) steaks halibut

½ cup white wine

1 teaspoon chopped garlic

¼ cup butter

salt and pepper to taste

3 tablespoons capers, with liquid

DIRECTIONS:

1

Heat the olive oil in a large skillet over medium-high heat. Fry the halibut steaks on all sides until nicely browned. Remove from pan, and set aside.

2

Pour the wine into the pan, and use a spatula to scrape any browned bits from the bottom. Let the wine reduce to almost nothing, then stir in the garlic, butter and capers. Season with salt and pepper to taste. Let the sauce simmer for a minute to blend the flavors.

3

Return the steaks to the pan, and coat them with sauce. Cook until fish flakes easily with a fork. Serve fish immediately with the sauce from the pan poured ov

NUTRITION FACTS:
284 calories; protein 24.2g; carbohydrates 1.4g; fat 17g;

AWESOME BROCCOLI MARINARA

Prep:
5 mins
Cook:
20 mins
Total:
25 mins
Servings:
4
Yield:
4 servings

INGREDIENTS:
2 tablespoons olive oil
1 (14.5 ounce) can diced tomatoes with balsamic vinegar, basil and olive oil
1 pound broccoli florets
2 cloves garlic, chopped
salt and pepper to taste

DIRECTIONS:
1

Heat olive oil in a large skillet over medium heat. Add garlic, and cook for a few minutes, stirring constantly. Pour in the tomatoes with their juices, and simmer until the liquid has reduced by about 1/2. Place the broccoli on top of the tomatoes, and season with a little salt and pepper. Cover, and simmer over low heat for 10 minutes, or until the broccoli is tender. Do not over cook the broccoli, it should be a vibrant green. Pour into a serving dish, and toss to blend with the sauce before serving.

NUTRITION FACTS:

122 calories; protein 4.1g; carbohydrates 11.4g; fat 7.2g;

GRILLED SEA BASS

Prep:

20 mins

Cook:

20 mins

Total:

40 mins

Servings:

6

Yield:

6 servings

INGREDIENTS:

¼ teaspoon garlic powder

¼ teaspoon onion powder

¼ teaspoon paprika

lemon pepper to taste

sea salt to taste

2 pounds sea bass

3 tablespoons butter

2 large cloves garlic, chopped

1 tablespoon chopped Italian flat leaf parsley

1 ½ tablespoons extra virgin olive oil

DIRECTIONS:

1

Preheat grill for high heat.

2

In a small bowl, stir together the garlic powder, onion powder, paprika, lemon pepper, and sea salt. Sprinkle seasonings onto the fish.

3

In a small saucepan over medium heat, melt the butter with the garlic and parsley. Remove from heat when the butter has melted, and set aside.

4

Lightly oil grill grate. Grill fish for 7 minutes, then turn and drizzle with butter. Continue cooking for 7 minutes, or until easily flaked with a fork. Drizzle with olive oil before serving.

NUTRITION FACTS:
232 calories; protein 28.2g; carbohydrates 0.8g; fat 12.2g;

TAMARIND SAUCE FISH CURRY

Prep:

15 mins

Cook:

25 mins

Additional:

10 mins

Total:

50 mins

Servings:

6

Yield:

6 servings

INGREDIENTS:

2 pounds white carp, cut into large chunks

1 tablespoon vegetable oil

1 tablespoon red chile powder

1 tablespoon ground turmeric

1 ½ teaspoons salt

¼ cup tamarind pulp

1 cup warm water

¼ cup oil

½ teaspoon cumin seeds

1 large onion, minced

1 ½ tablespoons garlic paste

2 tablespoons red chile powder

2 tablespoons ground coriander

1 pinch salt to taste

1 tablespoon chopped fresh coriander (cilantro), or to taste

DIRECTIONS:

1

Place fish in a bowl; add 1 tablespoon vegetable oil, 1 tablespoon chile powder, turmeric, and 1 1/2 teaspoons salt and allow to marinate for about 10 minutes.

2

Place tamarind pulp in a bowl and pour warm water over it. Squeeze tamarind to extract juice.

3

Heat 1/4 cup oil in a skillet over medium heat; add cumin seeds and stir. Add onion to cumin; cook and stir until onion is translucent, 5 to 10 minutes. Add garlic paste and cook for 3 minutes. Add carp, cover the skillet, and cook for 5 minutes.

4

Mix tamarind juice into fish mixture; bring to a boil. Turn carp pieces; add 2 tablespoons red chile powder, coriander, and salt. Cook over low heat until sauce thickens and oil separates, about 10 minutes. Garnish with coriander leaves.

NUTRITION FACTS:

360 calories; protein 28.4g; carbohydrates 12.5g; fat 21.1g;

CHAPTER 4: SNACK & APPETIZERS

BLISS BALLS

Prep:

30 mins

Additional:

40 mins

Total:

1 hr 10 mins

Servings:

30

Yield:

30 servings

INGREDIENTS:

2 ½ tablespoons flax seeds

1 cup almonds

¾ cup sesame seeds

½ cup sunflower seeds

½ cup cocoa nibs

¼ cup raw cocoa powder

3 tablespoons raw maca powder (Optional)

3 tablespoons chia seeds (Optional)

1 ½ teaspoons spirulina powder

1 teaspoon ground cardamom

¼ teaspoon ground cinnamon

1 pinch salt

1 cup Medjool dates, pitted

½ cup tahini

½ cup almond butter

⅓ cup honey

½ teaspoon vanilla extract

½ cup shredded unsweetened coconut

DIRECTIONS:

1

Soak flax seeds in a bowl of water for 10 minutes. Drain.

2

Blend almonds in a food processor or blender until finely chopped; transfer to a bowl. Mix sesame seeds, sunflower seeds, cocoa nibs, cocoa powder, maca powder, chia seeds, spirulina powder, cardamom, cinnamon, and salt into almonds.

3

Process dates in the food processor or blender; add to almond mixture.

4

Combine tahini, almond butter, honey, and vanilla extract in a separate bowl. Slowly mix almond mixture into tahini mixture until it holds together. Form mixture into bite-size balls.

5

Spread coconut in a shallow bowl. Roll the balls in the coconut until coated. Chill balls in the refrigerator, at least 30 minutes.

NUTRITION FACTS:

185 calories; protein 4.6g; carbohydrates 15.7g; fat 13g;

PESTO WITH ARAGULA

Prep:

15 mins

Total:

15 mins

Servings:

12

Yield:

12 servings

INGREDIENTS:

1 ½ cups baby arugula leaves

1 ½ cups fresh basil leaves

⅔ cup pine nuts

8 cloves garlic

1 (6 ounce) can black olives, drained

¾ cup extra virgin olive oil

½ lime, juiced

1 teaspoon red wine vinegar

⅛ teaspoon ground cumin

1 pinch ground cayenne pepper

salt and pepper to taste

DIRECTIONS:

1

Place the arugula, basil, pine nuts, garlic, and olives in a food processor, and chop to a coarse paste. Mix in olive oil, lime juice, vinegar, cumin, cayenne pepper, salt, and pepper. Process until well blended and smooth.

NUTRITION FACTS:

191 calories; protein 2.3g; carbohydrates 3.2g; fat 19.4g;

HOMEMADE SAUERKRAUT

Prep:
25 mins
Additional:
1 week
Total:
1 week
Servings:
24
Yield:
3 pounds of sauerkraut

INGREDIENTS:
5 pounds cabbage, thinly sliced
1 onion, thinly sliced
3 tablespoons sea salt
3 cloves garlic, minced, or more to taste
water to cover

DIRECTIONS:
1
Mix cabbage, onion, sea salt, and garlic together in a bowl. Firmly pack mixture into a large, clean, food-grade plastic bucket. The cabbage will start to make its own brine as the salt starts to draw out the water of the cabbage.

2
Fill a large, clean, food-grade plastic bag with water and place over the salted cabbage mixture so none of the cabbage is exposed to air.

3

Allow cabbage to ferment in a cool, dry place, 1 to 4 weeks (depending on how tangy you like your sauerkraut). The temperature of the room you ferment the sauerkraut in should not rise above 70 degrees F (21 degrees C).

NUTRITION FACTS:

28 calories; protein 1.3g; carbohydrates 6.5g; fat 0.1g;

ZUCCHINI TOTS

Prep:

10 mins

Cook:

15 mins

Total:

25 mins

Servings:

6

Yield:

12 tots

INGREDIENTS:

cooking spray

1 cup grated zucchini

¼ cup grated carrot

¼ cup seasoned bread crumbs

¼ cup crumbled feta cheese

¼ cup chopped fresh basil

1 egg

½ teaspoon salt

¼ teaspoon ground black pepper

⅛ teaspoon dried oregano

DIRECTIONS:

1

Preheat oven to 400 degrees F (200 degrees C). Spray a mini-muffin tin with cooking spray.

2

Combine zucchini and carrot in a large bowl. Squeeze out excess water using a paper towel.

3

Mix bread crumbs, feta cheese, basil, egg, salt, pepper, and oregano into zucchini-carrot mixture. Scoop mixture using a mini ice cream scoop or 2 spoons and press mixture into the prepared muffin tin using the back of a spoon.

4

Bake in the preheated oven until tops are golden brown, 15 to 18 minutes.

NUTRITION FACTS:
65 calories; protein 3.6g; carbohydrates 5.2g; fat 3.4g;

AVOCADO BASIL CUCUMBER BITES

Prep:

10 mins

Total:

10 mins

Servings:

4

Yield:

4 servings

INGREDIENTS:

1 ripe avocado, peeled and pitted

½ cup fresh basil leaves

1 tablespoon lime juice

1 clove garlic

¼ teaspoon salt

¼ teaspoon ground black pepper

1 cucumber, cut into 1/4-inch slices

1 plum tomato, cut into 1/4-inch slices

1 tablespoon plain yogurt, or to taste (Optional)

DIRECTIONS:

1

Blend avocado, basil, lime juice, garlic, salt, and pepper together in a food processor or blender until smooth.

2

Spread avocado mixture onto each cucumber slice and top with tomato slice and yogurt.

NUTRITION FACTS:
97 calories; protein 1.9g; carbohydrates 7.8g; fat 7.6g;

FURIKAKE SNACK MIX

Prep:

10 mins

Cook:

1 hr 5 mins

Additional:

30 mins

Total:

1 hr 45 mins

Servings:

20

Yield:

20 servings

INGREDIENTS:

½ cup butter

½ cup white sugar

½ cup corn oil

½ cup light corn syrup

2 (12 ounce) packages crispy corn and rice cereal

1 (1.9 ounce) container aji nori furikake (seasoned seaweed and sesame rice topping)

DIRECTIONS:

1

Preheat oven to 225 degrees F (110 degrees C).

2

Melt the butter and sugar together in a small sauce pan over low heat. Remove from heat, then stir in the corn oil and corn syrup. Place the cereal on a large baking sheet. Pour the butter mixture over the cereal, then sprinkle the furikake while tossing the cereal to coat.

3

Bake in the preheated oven until the cereal is dry, stirring every 15 minutes to keep cereal from browning too quickly. Allow to cool, then store in an airtight container.

NUTRITION FACTS:
274 calories; protein 2.5g; carbohydrates 43g; fat 10.7g;

BAKED BANANA CHIPS

Prep:

10 mins

Cook:

2 hrs

Additional:

5 mins

Total:

2 hrs 15 mins

Servings:

2

Yield:

2 bananas

INGREDIENTS:

2 just-ripe bananas, sliced in 1/10-inch-thick rounds, or more as needed

1 teaspoon lemon juice, or to taste

DIRECTIONS:

1

Preheat oven to 225 degrees F (110 degrees C). Line a baking sheet with parchment paper.

2

Spread banana slices out onto the prepared baking sheet, making sure slices are not touching. Brush slices with lemon juice.

3

Bake in the preheated oven for 90 minutes. Check bananas, lifting slices up to separate from the paper once or twice. Continue baking until bananas are dried out, 30 to 90 minutes more.

4

Let bananas cool until crispy, at least 5 minutes.

NUTRITION FACTS:

106 calories; protein 1.3g; carbohydrates 27.2g; fat 0.4g;

TROPICAL FRUIT SANDWICH

Prep:
15 mins
Total:
15 mins
Servings:
8
Yield:
8 sandwiches

INGREDIENTS:
1 (8 ounce) package Neufchatel cheese, softened
¼ cup crushed pineapple, drained
4 bananas, sliced
½ cup shredded coconut
16 slices whole-grain bread

DIRECTIONS:
  1
In a small bowl, mix together softened Neufchatel cheese and
pineapple.

  2
Spread cheese mixture on one slice of bread, top with slices of
banana and a sprinkling of coconut, and top with another slice of
bread to make a sandwich. Repeat with remaining ingredients.

NUTRITION FACTS:
289 calories; protein 10.6g; carbohydrates 40.4g; fat 10.3g;

CHAPTER 5: DESSERT

MANGO SALAD

Prep:

20 mins

Total:

20 mins

Servings:

4

Yield:

4 servings

INGREDIENTS:

2 firm green mangoes - peeled, pitted, and cut into matchsticks

¼ purple onion, thinly sliced

¼ red bell pepper, thinly sliced

3 sprigs cilantro, or more to taste, leaves removed and stems discarded

2 tablespoons lime juice

2 tablespoons fish sauce

1 tablespoon brown sugar

1 tablespoon crushed peanuts

DIRECTIONS:

1

Mix mangoes, onion, red bell pepper, and cilantro leaves together in a bowl.

2

Whisk lime juice, fish sauce, and brown sugar together in a separate bowl until the sugar is dissolved; pour over the mango mixture and toss to coat. Top salad with peanuts.

NUTRITION FACTS:
84 calories; protein 1.5g; carbohydrates 18.6g; fat 1.3g;

FIG NEWTON-ISH COOKIES

Prep:
1 hr
Cook:
40 mins
Additional:
12 hrs 55 mins
Total:
14 hrs 35 mins
Servings:
18
Yield:
18 servings

INGREDIENTS:
Cookie Dough:
¾ cup whole wheat flour
½ cup finely ground walnuts
¾ teaspoon baking soda
¼ teaspoon salt
¼ teaspoon ground cinnamon
⅛ teaspoon ground nutmeg
¼ cup unsalted butter, softened
3 tablespoons brown sugar
2 tablespoons honey
1 large egg
¼ teaspoon grated orange zest
1 teaspoon vanilla extract

Fig Filling:

1 cup dried figs

½ cup water

4 tablespoons honey, or to taste

1 orange, juiced

1 teaspoon vanilla extract

½ teaspoon grated orange zest

¼ teaspoon ground nutmeg

1 pinch salt

DIRECTIONS:

1

Combine whole wheat flour, ground walnuts, baking soda, salt, cinnamon, and nutmeg in a medium bowl.

2

Beat butter, brown sugar, and honey together in a large bowl until light and fluffy. Add egg, orange zest, and vanilla extract; beat until thoroughly combined. Add flour mixture in 3 batches, mixing until just combined and dough is very soft and sticky.

3

Wrap dough in plastic wrap. Pat into a disk and refrigerate, 4 hours to overnight.

4

Place figs, water, honey, orange juice, vanilla extract, orange zest, and nutmeg in a medium saucepan. Bring filling mixture to a simmer over medium heat, stirring occasionally. Cook until figs are softened and fall apart easily when pressed with a spoon, about 15 minutes. Remove from heat and cool for 10 minutes.

5

Place filling mixture into a blender or food processor and puree until smooth. Pour puree into a glass container and let cool completely until filling has a spreadable consistency. Refrigerate until ready to use.

6

Preheat the oven to 350 degrees F (175 degrees C).

7

Place a piece of parchment paper on a work surface and generously flour the paper and a rolling pin. Roll out the chilled cookie dough into a 10x14-inch rectangle about 1/4 inch thick. Continue to flour the parchment and rolling pin as necessary. Divide dough into 4 strips about 3 1/2 inches wide by 10 inches long.

8

Divide the fig filling among the strips of dough. Spread filling lengthwise down the center of each piece, leaving about 1/2 inch of space on the sides. Gently pull one side of the dough halfway over the filling. Repeat with the opposite side and pinch to seal in the filling to form a cookie log about 1 inch wide and 10 inches long.

9

Gently roll the log over so it's seam-side down. Brush off any excess flour and gently press the top of the roll to flatten slightly. Repeat this process with the other dough strips.

10

Brush off any excess flour from the top of, and in between, the cookie logs. Gently lift the parchment paper, with the cookies still on it, onto a baking sheet. Arrange logs about 1 inch apart on the baking sheet.

11

Bake in the preheated oven until cookies just begin to brown and feel slightly crispy to the touch, 20 to 25 minutes. Let cookies cool for 5 minutes. Use a serrated knife to slice each log into 8 pieces about 1 1/4 inch long and 1 inch wide. Let cookies cool completely, at least 40 minutes.

12

Store cooled cookies in an airtight container until softened, 8 hours to overnight.

NUTRITION FACTS:
119 calories; protein 1.8g; carbohydrates 19.5g; fat 4.5g;

CINNAMON COFFEE CAKE

Servings:
14
Yield:
1 -10 inch tube

INGREDIENTS:
1 cup butter
2 ¾ cups white sugar
4 large eggs
2 teaspoons baking powder
1 teaspoon baking soda
1 teaspoon salt
2 cups sour cream
1 ½ cups chopped walnuts
2 tablespoons ground cinnamon
2 teaspoons vanilla extract
4 cups all-purpose flour

DIRECTIONS:
   1
Preheat oven to 350 degrees F (175 degrees C). Lightly grease one 10 inch tube pan.

   2
In a large mixing bowl cream together the butter or margarine and 2 cups of the sugar until fluffy. Add the vanilla and the eggs one at time beating mixture well after each egg.

3

Combine flour with baking powder, baking soda, and salt. Add alternately with sour cream to egg mixture. Beating just enough after each addition to keep batter smooth.

4

Combine walnuts, cinnamon, and remaining 3/4 cup of sugar.

5

Spoon 1/3 of the batter into prepared pan, sprinkle with 1/3 of the walnut mixture. Repeat layers two more times.

6

Bake at 350 degrees F (175 degrees C) for 70 minutes or until center is done. Let cake cool in pan for 10 minutes then remove pan and let cake continue cooling on a wire rack.

NUTRITION FACTS:
576 calories; protein 8.6g; carbohydrates 70.8g; fat 30g;

CARAMEL

Prep:

15 mins

Cook:

45 mins

Total:

1 hr

Servings:

16

Yield:

4 cups

INGREDIENTS:

3 cups white sugar

1 ½ cups corn syrup

1 pinch salt

2 cups liquid non-dairy creamer

½ teaspoon vanilla extract

DIRECTIONS:

1

In a heavy bottomed saucepan, combine sugar, corn syrup, salt and 1 cup non-dairy creamer. Heat to between 234 and 240 degrees F (112 to 116 degrees C), or until a small amount of syrup dropped into cold water forms a soft ball that flattens when removed from the water and placed on a flat surface.

2

Combine vanilla and remaining creamer and stir, a little at a time, into caramel. For a soft caramel, remove from heat and pour into a buttered 8x8 inch dish. For a hard candy or caramel apple coating, continue cooking until mixture reaches hard ball stage, 250 to 265 degrees F (121 to 129 degrees C), or until a small amount of syrup dropped into cold water forms a rigid ball.

NUTRITION FACTS:

273 calories; protein 0.3g; carbohydrates 64.5g; fat 3g;

BAKED BANANAS

Prep:
10 mins
Cook:
10 mins
Total:
20 mins
Servings:
4
Yield:
4 servings

INGREDIENTS:
cooking spray
4 firm bananas, peeled and halved lengthwise
¼ cup maple syrup (Optional)
1 tablespoon ground cinnamon
1 (1 inch) piece fresh ginger, grated
1 ½ teaspoons ground nutmeg

DIRECTIONS:
1
Preheat oven to 375 degrees F (190 degrees C). Spray a baking dish with cooking spray.

2
Arrange banana halves in the prepared baking dish. Drizzle maple syrup over bananas and top with cinnamon, ginger, and nutmeg. Cover dish with aluminum foil.

3

Bake in the preheated oven until heated through, 10 to 15 minutes.

NUTRITION FACTS:

168 calories; protein 1.4g; carbohydrates 42.4g; fat 0.9g;

BANANA CREPES

Prep:

5 mins

Cook:

15 mins

Total:

20 mins

Servings:

6

Yield:

6 servings

INGREDIENTS:

1 cup all-purpose flour

¼ cup confectioners' sugar

2 eggs

1 cup milk

3 tablespoons butter, melted

1 teaspoon vanilla extract

¼ teaspoon salt

¼ cup butter

¼ cup packed brown sugar

¼ teaspoon ground cinnamon

¼ teaspoon ground nutmeg

¼ cup half-and-half cream

6 bananas, halved lengthwise

1 ½ cups whipped heavy cream

1 pinch ground cinnamon

DIRECTIONS:

1

Sift flour and powdered sugar into a mixing bowl. Add eggs, milk, butter, vanilla, and salt; beat until smooth.

2

Heat a lightly greased 6 inch skillet. Add about 3 tablespoons batter. Tilt skillet so that batter spreads to almost cover the bottom of skillet. Cook until lightly browned; turn and brown the other side. Repeat process with remaining batter, grease skillet as needed.

3

Melt 1/4 cup butter in a large skillet. Stir in brown sugar, 1/4 teaspoon cinnamon and nutmeg. Stir in cream and cook until slightly thickened. Add half the bananas at a time to skillet; cook for 2 to 3 minutes, spooning sauce over them. Remove from heat.

4

Roll a crepe around each banana half and place on serving platter. Spoon sauce over crepes. Top with whipped cream and a pinch of cinnamon.

NUTRITION FACTS:
519 calories; protein 8g; carbohydrates 60.7g; fat 28.7g;

PUMPKIN DONUTS

Prep:

15 mins

Cook:

15 mins

Total:

30 mins

Servings:

12

Yield:

12 doughnuts

DIRECTIONS:

2 cups all-purpose flour

½ cup brown sugar

2 teaspoons pumpkin pie spice

1 ½ teaspoons baking powder

½ teaspoon salt

¼ teaspoon baking soda

¾ cup pumpkin puree

2 eggs

¼ cup milk

¼ cup butter, softened

Icing:

1 cup confectioners' sugar, sifted

¼ teaspoon vanilla extract

½ teaspoon pumpkin pie spice

4 teaspoons milk, or as needed

DIRECTIONS:

1

Preheat oven to 375 degrees F (190 degrees C). Lightly grease 2 baking sheets.

2

Stir flour, brown sugar, 2 teaspoons pumpkin pie spice, baking powder, salt, and baking soda together in a large bowl.

3

Mix pumpkin, eggs, milk, and butter into flour mixture; beat until completely incorporated.

4

Spoon pumpkin mixture into a pastry bag fitted with a large star tip with a 1/2-inch opening. Pipe 3-inch circles onto prepared baking sheets.

5

Bake in the preheated oven until golden brown, about 13 minutes. Remove doughnuts to a wire rack to cool.

6

Stir confectioner's sugar, 1/2 teaspoon pumpkin pie spice, and vanilla together in a bowl. Gradually stir in enough milk to reach a glaze consistency. Brush glaze over doughnuts with a pastry brush or spoon over the tops.

NUTRITION FACTS:

205 calories; protein 3.5g; carbohydrates 37.2g; fat 5g;

CHEWY COCONUT COOKIES

Prep:

30 mins

Cook:

10 mins

Additional:

10 mins

Total:

50 mins

Servings:

36

Yield:

3 dozen

INGREDIENTS:

1 ¼ cups all-purpose flour

½ teaspoon baking soda

¼ teaspoon salt

½ cup butter

½ cup packed brown sugar

½ cup white sugar

1 egg

½ teaspoon vanilla extract

1 ⅓ cups flaked coconut

DIRECTIONS:

1

Preheat oven to 350 degrees F (175 degrees C.) Combine the flour, baking soda, and salt; set aside.

2

In a medium bowl, cream the butter, brown sugar, and white sugar until smooth. Beat in the egg and vanilla until light and fluffy. Gradually blend in the flour mixture, then mix in the coconut. Drop dough by teaspoonfuls onto an ungreased cookie sheet. Cookies should be about 3 inches apart.

3

Bake for 8 to 10 minutes in the preheated oven, or until lightly toasted. Cool on wire racks.

NUTRITION FACTS:

75 calories; protein 0.7g; carbohydrates 10.5g; fat 3.5g;

CPSIA information can be obtained
at www.ICGtesting.com
Printed in the USA
BVHW010846150621
609627BV00002B/92